CONTENTS

What can astrology do for me? 2

What is astrology? 4

Your Sun sign 10

Your Rising sign 20

Your Moon sign 28

Elements 38

We are family 44

Best of friends 54

Your birthday log 64

Lucky in love 78

Life at school 86

WHAT CAN ASTROLOGY
do for me?

Astrology is a powerful tool for self-awareness. The idea that we are all connected – that the shifting energies of the Sun, Moon and planets above affect us here on Earth – is an ancient and philosophical belief. Astrology isn't fortune-telling – it can't predict your future and it doesn't deal in absolutes. It simply says that you are part of the universe around you, and by studying the stars, it's possible to learn more about yourself.

Why is this so important? Because the better understanding you have of your own inner make-up – your skills, your talents, your needs and your fears – the more insight you gain into why you act the way you do. And this gives you choices, empowering you to make changes and to build on your strengths. It makes it easier to feel confident and to accept yourself, quirks and all.

There are countless daily horoscopes in newspapers, magazines and online. But this book looks at more than just your star sign, which is only a small part of your personality picture. It helps you to find your Rising sign, which was appearing over the Eastern horizon at the time of your birth, and has a lot to tell you about the way others see you. You can also work out your Moon sign, which reveals the real you deep down inside, giving you the chance to get to grips with your innermost emotions, desires, fears and obsessions.

With a clearer picture of who you are, life becomes less complicated. Instead of trying to live up to others' expectations and being someone you're not, you can work instead on becoming the best version of yourself possible – someone who understands their talents and needs, who is perfectly unique and is happy.

What is
ASTROLOGY?

The stars and planets have always inspired a sense of wonder. The ancient peoples of Babylonia, Persia, Egypt, Greece and India were all fascinated by the cycles of the Moon, the rising and setting of the Sun, the position of the constellations and what it all meant. As these civilizations developed, they connected what they saw in the sky with the people and events on Earth, and astrology was born.

In ancient times, astrology was used to help monarchs rule. Kings and emperors would employ astrologers to predict the weather, speak to the gods and help manage the country.

Modern astrology has evolved to help ordinary people like you and me understand ourselves better – how we behave, how we feel about each other and how we can make the best of who we are.

THE SIGNS OF THE ZODIAC

Today we know that the planets revolve around the Sun, but astrology is based on how we see the solar system from here on Earth. The Zodiac is a group of 12 constellations that, from our viewpoint, seem to rotate around Earth over the course of a year, like a huge wheel. These constellations are named after the animals and objects that our ancestors thought they looked most like – the ram, the lion, the scorpion and so on. Your Sun sign tells you which of the constellations the Sun was moving through on the day you were born. The signs have a natural order that never varies, beginning with Aries. The dates given on the right change slightly from year to year for the same reasons we have a leap year – each of our days is slightly longer than 24 hours. If you were born at the beginning or end of a sign, called 'the cusp', it's worth checking your Sun sign online to be sure.

ARIES
March 21–April 20

TAURUS
April 21–May 21

GEMINI
May 22–June 21

CANCER
June 22–July 22

LEO
July 23–August 23

VIRGO
August 24–September 22

LIBRA
September 23–October 22

SCORPIO
October 23–November 21

SAGITTARIUS
November 22–December 21

CAPRICORN
December 22–January 20

AQUARIUS
January 21–February 19

PISCES
February 20–March 20

THE FOUR ELEMENTS

*Each Sun sign is associated with one of four elements –
Fire, Earth, Air and Water.*

FIRE

Aries, Leo, Sagittarius
Fire signs are passionate, dynamic and temperamental.
They mix well with: Fire and Air types

EARTH

Taurus, Virgo, Capricorn
Earth signs are practical, cautious and reliable.
They mix well with: Water and Earth types

AIR

Gemini, Libra, Aquarius
Air signs are quick, curious and adventurous.
They mix well with: Air and Fire types

WATER

Cancer, Scorpio, Pisces
Water signs are sensitive, emotional and kind.
They mix well with: Earth and Water types

THE PLANETS

Astrology looks at the positions of the stars and planets at the time and place of your birth. The Sun and Moon aren't technically planets, but they're referred to that way by astrologers for ease of use. The Sun is a great place to start – it's the most important object in the solar system. Your Sun sign describes the essence of your identity and says a great deal about your potential – the person you might become.

The position the Moon held in the sky at the time of your birth has a strong influence, too. It describes your emotions – how you feel deep inside. It can give you a better understanding of what you need to feel loved and cared for.

And there's also your Rising sign. This is the sign of the Zodiac that was appearing over the Eastern horizon at the time of your birth. It tells you more about how you interact with the world around you, especially to new situations. It's the filter through which you perceive the world and the impression you give to others on first meeting. Which means it's also how others often see you.

The positions of the other planets – Venus, Mercury, Mars, etc – in your birth chart all have their own effect. But these three taken together – Sun, Moon and Rising sign – will give you a deeper understanding of who you are and what you could become, your strengths and weaknesses, your real self.

Your SUN sign

CAPRICORN

December 22–January 20

SYMBOL
The Sea-Goat

ELEMENT
Earth

RULING PLANET
Saturn

BIRTHSTONE
Garnet

COLOUR
Brown

BODY PART
Knees, bones, teeth

DAY OF THE WEEK
Saturday

FLOWER
Pansy

CHARACTER TRAITS
Ambitious, responsible, determined

KEY PHRASE
'I use'

YOUR SUN SIGN

When people talk about astrology and ask about your star sign, they're referring to your Sun sign. It tells you which of the 12 constellations of the Zodiac the Sun was moving through on the day you were born. This makes it easy to work out, which is one of the reasons for its popularity. If you'd like to know the Sun sign of a friend or family member, the table on page 7 shows which days the Sun occupies each of the signs over the course of a year.

The Sun is the heart of your chart – it's the essence of who you are and symbolizes the potential of what you can achieve. It's important to remember, though, that it is only a part of the whole picture when it comes to astrology. It's a wonderful starting point, but there are many other layers encasing your core identity, all of which affect the inner you.

ALL ABOUT YOU

Born with the Sun in Capricorn, you have the potential to inspire others to achieve their dreams – your desire to do your absolute best in everything you undertake is hugely motivating to those around you. You are goal-oriented and are prepared to work hard to get to where you want to be – no matter how long it takes. Financial security is important to you.

Wise beyond your years, your old soul might mean you occasionally feel out of sync with what your classmates find important. But when you do make a connection with someone, you love to hang out as often as you can. Luckily, your friends' parents always welcome you with open arms thanks to your perfect manners.

You're not particularly spontaneous, preferring to follow a set routine, and you're naturally cautious. Don't worry: it doesn't mean you're boring – in fact, you have a hidden silly streak that is hugely infectious and probably makes your close friends cry with laughter.

Likes

Structure
Older friends
Feeling prepared
Working
Being in charge

Dislikes

Taking risks
Vulnerability
Failing

HOW TO BRING OUT YOUR BEST

From an early age, you've understood what makes you tick. However, you have a reluctance to talk about your feelings. This means you can come across as secretive and 'matter-of-fact' around your friends. After all, they want to get to know all they can about you. You don't have to reveal all your innermost thoughts, but sharing can help build bonds of trust. You have a warm heart that only a special few really get to see.

If something doesn't go to plan, your strong sense of responsibility means you often blame yourself – even when it wasn't your fault. Listening to a close friend's view of the situation can give you a fairer perspective.

You can become frustrated with friends when they don't pick things up as quickly as you – perhaps you're playing a new game, for instance, and they're just not getting it. Part of your journey is acceptance: not everyone is as sharp as you.

Strengths

Determined
Focused
Trustworthy
Fair
Responsible
Patient
Funny

Weaknesses

Bossy
Uptight
Critical

SECRET FEARS

If any Zodiac sign can achieve their dreams, it's you. That's because you are prepared to put in the hard work that's required and don't believe in quitting. However, deep down, you can doubt your ability. Everyone needs reassurance when they're struggling, so don't be afraid to ask for it. Your friends will be only too happy to sing your praises.

You can be surprisingly sensitive for someone who appears so at ease with yourself, and throwaway comments can hurt your feelings. Don't let these fester: far better to have a quick chat with whoever said it and then put it behind you.

Most likely to . . .

Plan (way) ahead

Offer advice

Suffer in silence

Never give up

Think you're right

Remember the details

Play it safe

Reach the top

YOUR RISING SIGN

Your Rising sign, also known as your Ascendant, is the sign that was rising over the Eastern horizon (the place where the Sun rises each day) when you were born. It describes how you see the world and the people around you and how they see you – the first impression that you give and receive, the image you project, and the initial reaction you might have to a new situation. A person with Leo Rising, for example, may strike you as warm and engaging, whereas Pisces Rising is more sensitive and possibly shy. Because the Ascendant is determined by the exact time and place you were born, it is the most personal point in your chart. Many astrologers believe this makes it just as important as your Sun sign.

HOW TO FIND YOUR ASCENDANT

This is where it gets a bit tricky. There's a reason that popular astrology only deals with your Sun sign – your Rising sign can be more difficult to work out. But don't be put off. If you know your Sun sign and your time of birth, you can use the table on the right to give you a good idea. To be totally accurate you do need to take into account factors like time zone and daylight savings, and there are plenty of free online calculators that will do just that.

YOUR SUN SIGN	YOUR HOUR OF BIRTH											
	6:00 AM to 8:00 AM	8:00 AM to 10:00 AM	10:00 AM to 12:00 PM	12:00 PM to 2:00 PM	2:00 PM to 4:00 PM	4:00 PM to 6:00 PM	6:00 PM to 8:00 PM	8:00 PM to 10:00 PM	10:00 PM to 12:00 AM	12:00 AM to 2:00 AM	2:00 AM to 4:00 AM	4:00 AM to 6:00 AM
ARIES ♈	♉	♊	♋	♌	♍	♎	♏	♐	♑	♒	♓	♈
TAURUS ♉	♊	♋	♌	♍	♎	♏	♐	♑	♒	♓	♈	♉
GEMINI ♊	♋	♌	♍	♎	♏	♐	♑	♒	♓	♈	♉	♊
CANCER ♋	♌	♍	♎	♏	♐	♑	♒	♓	♈	♉	♊	♋
LEO ♌	♍	♎	♏	♐	♑	♒	♓	♈	♉	♊	♋	♌
VIRGO ♍	♎	♏	♐	♑	♒	♓	♈	♉	♊	♋	♌	♍
LIBRA ♎	♏	♐	♑	♒	♓	♈	♉	♊	♋	♌	♍	♎
SCORPIO ♏	♐	♑	♒	♓	♈	♉	♊	♋	♌	♍	♎	♏
SAGITTARIUS ♐	♑	♒	♓	♈	♉	♊	♋	♌	♍	♎	♏	♐
CAPRICORN ♑	♒	♓	♈	♉	♊	♋	♌	♍	♎	♏	♐	♑
AQUARIUS ♒	♓	♈	♉	♊	♋	♌	♍	♎	♏	♐	♑	♒
PISCES ♓	♈	♉	♊	♋	♌	♍	♎	♏	♐	♑	♒	♓

WHAT YOUR RISING SIGN SAYS ABOUT YOU

Once you have figured out your Ascendant, you are ready to discover more about how you see the world, and how it sees you.

ARIES RISING

When Aries partners with Capricorn, the result can be intense. 'Laid-back' isn't in your vocabulary – you believe there's no time to spare. You're the classmate whose diary is filled with homework deadlines months ahead. While friends may tease you about this love of being organized, they often pick up tips to smooth over their own lives. Your will to succeed is formidable, and there's little you can't achieve as long as you balance your need for organization with your tendency to jump in feet first.

TAURUS RISING

The methodical Taurean approach takes the edge off Capricorn's competitive nature. An earthy combination, you are stable and dependable, happy to be yourself and forge your own path. You come across as calm and collected, and your appearance is important to you. Problems only arise when you're expected to embrace the new or unexpected. Your friends are only too happy to help, but you can find it hard to accept their kindness. Remember that it takes courage and strength to admit when you need back up – it's not a sign of weakness.

GEMINI RISING

A Gemini ascendant gives you a natural curiosity about the world around you and takes your communication skills up a notch. This pairing can be hugely successful – you have the imagination to come up with ideas and the stability to put them into action. Outwardly you are fun and outgoing, capable of fitting into any social situation. Internally you are practical and methodical, accepting of others and ready to put in the work required to achieve success.

CANCER RISING

Your sensitive outer shell belies your down-to-earth nature. Sweet and empathetic, you wear your heart on your sleeve and easily tune into the feelings of others. You feel happiest and most secure when you're working hard towards achieving something. Home is important to you, and you are most comfortable there – you put lots of energy into your family relationships. Easily hurt, you have a tendency to retreat when things get tough. Letting go of negative experiences rather than dwelling on them is one of your life challenges.

LEO RISING

Adding a dash of Leo to Capricorn brings an outer confidence tempered with humbleness. You fly through school exams because you pride yourself on being prepared. Yet when those top grades come flooding in, you find it hard to accept the congratulations you receive from your friends and family. While this modesty is commendable, it's okay to bask a little in your success – you've earned it! You're likely to be an inspirational leader once you enter the world of work. That Leo warmth and strong inner work ethic will bring out the best in any team.

VIRGO RISING

A savvy character who doesn't miss a trick, you are a problem solver with a cool approach. Friends are drawn to your level-headedness – you have a wisdom beyond your years which they know they can depend upon. Your health and physical appearance are important to you – you're happiest when you're eating well and exercising regularly. Your good memory and excellent attention to detail mean you're well suited to learning specialized skills, whether that's in medicine, industry or the arts.

LIBRA RISING

With Libra Rising, patience is second nature. You have the staying power to see situations and challenges through to the end. Creative and quick, you catch onto new ideas fast, and with an eye for design, you are usually the one leading the way when it comes to style trends. You love socializing, have a diplomatic approach that makes you popular with your friends and you tend to see the best in everyone – just be wary of those who might take advantage of your openness.

SCORPIO RISING

Scorpio brings with it an air of mystery. You don't trust people easily and can come across as reserved, with an unknowable quality that's magnetic and alluring. Friends who are invited into your inner circle soon realize just how loyal and trustworthy you are, though. You hate to let people down, and when it comes to your responsibilities, you step up. You see failure as a way to learn, and obstacles only serve to make you more determined to accomplish your goals.

SAGITTARIUS RISING

High-minded and idealistic, you're concerned with life's big questions and prefer not to bother with the smaller details. When it comes to broadening your understanding of the way the world works, your enthusiasm knows no bounds. Lively and sociable, you value your independence and won't be fenced in. You work well in groups and can be the life of the party. Channelling your vision and optimism into practical projects can yield great results.

CAPRICORN RISING

Twice a Capricorn, the essence of your inner self matches the way you deal with others. This gives you twice the drive to do the best you possibly can. Goal driven and an excellent planner, you are likely to be successful at whatever you set your mind to. You can't bear to cut corners, and while this is an admirable attitude, it can mean that classmates view you as a little serious from time to time. Hanging out with friends with a more laid-back attitude will help you to see that things work out perfectly well even if they're not perfect.

AQUARIUS RISING

This interesting combination can go one of two ways. At its best, you are fearlessly original, combining practical drive with daring innovation. At its worst, you run the risk of doggedly pursuing unrealistic, grandiose goals. Learn to keep things light-hearted, and find time to relax. Family-oriented, you have a sunny, joyful manner, and people are drawn to your witty remarks and clever ideas. Just be careful not to impose your opinions too fiercely on others.

PISCES RISING

Serious and dreamy in equal measure, you are quiet and possibly shy, yet possess a natural talent for making other people feel at ease. You have a wide social circle as a result, but you need to choose your friends wisely or they may take advantage. Learning to finish what you start is one of your biggest challenges – you have the inner drive and organizational skills but only when you focus. You can make a real difference to the world around you when you channel your intuition into practical enterprises.

Your MOON sign

YOUR MOON SIGN

The Moon rules your emotions and your inner moods, telling you what you need to feel safe, comfortable and loved. Knowing your Moon sign should give you a more complete picture of your unique self, helping you to express needs you might be struggling to understand. Suppose your Sun sign is Aries but being first has never been important to you – a Moon in Virgo may be telling you to hang back and fade into the background. Or you might have the Sun in home-loving Cancer but feel an urge to get out there and see the world. Perhaps that's because your Moon is in freedom-loving Sagittarius.

HOW TO FIND YOUR MOON SIGN

Just like your Rising sign, finding your Moon sign is more complicated than finding your Sun sign. That's because the Moon seems to move so quickly, taking just about a month to pass through all of the constellations. Thankfully, the tables on the right and on the next page make finding it a simple process.

First, find your year of birth. Then locate your birth month at the top of the table. Find your date of birth in the column below it, and this will give you your Moon sign. If your date of birth isn't listed, the one before it is your Moon sign.

For example, suppose your date of birth is 4 March, 1995. The date before this is 2 March, for which the Moon sign is Aries. This would mean your Moon sign is Aries.

JAN	FEB	MAR	APR	MAY	JUN	JUL	AUG	SEP	OCT	NOV	DEC
BORN IN THE YEAR 1995											
2 Aqu	1 Pis	2 Ari	1 Tau	1 Gem	2 Leo	2 Vir	3 Sco	1 Sag	2 Aqu	1 Pis	3 Tau
4 Pis	3 Ari	5 Tau	3 Gem	3 Can	5 Vir	4 Lib	5 Sag	3 Cap	5 Pis	3 Ari	5 Gem
7 Ari	5 Tau	7 Gem	6 Can	6 Leo	7 Lib	6 Sco	7 Cap	5 Aqu	7 Ari	5 Tau	8 Can
9 Tau	8 Gem	10 Can	9 Leo	8 Vir	9 Sco	8 Sag	9 Aqu	7 Pis	9 Tau	8 Gem	10 Leo
12 Gem	10 Can	12 Leo	11 Vir	10 Lib	11 Sag	10 Cap	11 Pis	9 Ari	12 Gem	10 Can	13 Vir
14 Can	13 Leo	14 Vir	13 Lib	13 Sco	13 Cap	12 Aqu	13 Ari	12 Tau	14 Can	13 Leo	15 Lib
16 Leo	15 Vir	17 Lib	15 Sco	15 Sag	15 Aqu	14 Pis	15 Tau	14 Gem	17 Leo	15 Vir	17 Sco
19 Vir	17 Lib	19 Sco	17 Sag	17 Cap	17 Pis	17 Ari	18 Gem	17 Can	19 Vir	18 Lib	19 Sag
21 Lib	19 Sco	21 Sag	19 Cap	19 Aqu	19 Ari	19 Tau	20 Can	19 Leo	21 Lib	20 Sco	21 Cap
23 Sco	22 Sag	23 Cap	21 Aqu	21 Pis	22 Tau	22 Gem	23 Leo	22 Vir	23 Sco	22 Sag	23 Aqu
25 Sag	24 Cap	25 Aqu	24 Pis	23 Ari	24 Gem	24 Can	25 Vir	24 Lib	26 Sag	24 Cap	25 Pis
27 Cap	26 Aqu	27 Pis	26 Ari	26 Tau	27 Can	27 Leo	28 Lib	26 Sco	28 Cap	26 Aqu	28 Ari
30 Aqu	28 Pis	30 Ari	28 Tau	28 Gem	29 Leo	29 Vir	30 Sco	28 Sag	30 Aqu	28 Pis	30 Tau
				31 Can		31 Lib		30 Cap		30 Ari	
BORN IN THE YEAR 1996											
1 Gem	3 Leo	1 Leo	2 Lib	2 Sco	2 Cap	2 Aqu	2 Ari	1 Tau	3 Can	2 Leo	2 Vir
4 Can	5 Vir	3 Vir	4 Sco	4 Sag	4 Aqu	4 Pis	4 Tau	3 Gem	5 Leo	4 Vir	4 Lib
6 Leo	8 Lib	6 Lib	7 Sag	6 Cap	6 Pis	6 Ari	6 Gem	6 Can	8 Vir	7 Lib	6 Sco
9 Vir	10 Sco	8 Sco	9 Cap	8 Aqu	9 Ari	8 Tau	9 Can	8 Leo	10 Lib	9 Sco	9 Sag
11 Lib	12 Sag	10 Sag	11 Aqu	10 Pis	11 Tau	11 Gem	11 Leo	11 Vir	13 Sco	11 Sag	11 Cap
14 Sco	14 Cap	13 Cap	13 Pis	12 Ari	13 Gem	13 Can	14 Vir	13 Lib	15 Sag	13 Cap	13 Aqu
16 Sag	16 Aqu	15 Aqu	15 Ari	15 Tau	16 Can	16 Leo	17 Lib	15 Sco	17 Cap	16 Aqu	15 Pis
18 Cap	18 Pis	17 Pis	17 Tau	17 Gem	18 Leo	18 Vir	19 Sco	18 Sag	19 Aqu	18 Pis	17 Ari
20 Aqu	20 Ari	19 Ari	20 Gem	19 Can	21 Vir	21 Lib	21 Sag	20 Cap	21 Pis	20 Ari	19 Tau
22 Pis	23 Tau	21 Tau	22 Can	22 Leo	23 Lib	23 Sco	24 Cap	22 Aqu	23 Ari	22 Tau	22 Gem
24 Ari	25 Gem	23 Gem	25 Leo	25 Vir	26 Sco	25 Sag	26 Aqu	24 Pis	26 Tau	24 Gem	24 Can
26 Tau	27 Can	26 Can	27 Vir	27 Lib	28 Sag	27 Cap	28 Pis	26 Ari	28 Gem	27 Can	26 Leo
29 Gem		28 Leo	30 Lib	29 Sco	30 Cap	29 Aqu	30 Ari	28 Tau	30 Can	29 Leo	29 Vir
31 Can		31 Vir		31 Sag		31 Pis		30 Gem			31 Lib
BORN IN THE YEAR 1997											
3 Sco	1 Sag	1 Sag	1 Aqu	1 Pis	1 Tau	1 Gem	2 Leo	3 Lib	3 Sco	1 Sag	1 Cap
5 Sag	4 Cap	3 Cap	4 Pis	3 Ari	4 Gem	3 Can	4 Vir	6 Sco	5 Sag	4 Cap	3 Aqu
7 Cap	6 Aqu	5 Aqu	6 Ari	5 Tau	6 Can	5 Leo	7 Lib	8 Sag	8 Cap	6 Aqu	5 Pis
9 Aqu	8 Pis	7 Pis	8 Tau	7 Gem	8 Leo	8 Vir	9 Sco	10 Cap	10 Aqu	8 Pis	8 Ari
11 Pis	10 Ari	9 Ari	10 Gem	9 Can	11 Vir	10 Lib	12 Sag	12 Aqu	12 Pis	10 Ari	10 Tau
13 Ari	12 Tau	11 Tau	12 Can	12 Leo	13 Lib	13 Sco	14 Cap	15 Pis	14 Ari	12 Tau	12 Gem
15 Tau	14 Gem	13 Gem	14 Leo	14 Vir	16 Sco	15 Sag	16 Aqu	17 Ari	16 Tau	14 Gem	14 Can
18 Gem	16 Can	16 Can	17 Vir	17 Lib	18 Sag	18 Cap	18 Pis	19 Tau	18 Gem	17 Can	16 Leo
20 Can	19 Leo	18 Leo	19 Lib	19 Sco	20 Cap	20 Aqu	20 Ari	21 Gem	20 Can	19 Leo	19 Vir
23 Leo	21 Vir	21 Vir	22 Sco	22 Sag	22 Aqu	22 Pis	22 Tau	23 Can	23 Leo	21 Vir	21 Lib
25 Vir	24 Lib	23 Lib	24 Sag	24 Cap	24 Pis	24 Ari	24 Gem	25 Leo	25 Vir	24 Lib	24 Sco
28 Lib	26 Sco	26 Sco	27 Cap	26 Aqu	26 Ari	26 Tau	27 Can	28 Vir	28 Lib	26 Sco	26 Sag
30 Sco		28 Sag	29 Aqu	28 Pis	28 Tau	28 Gem	29 Leo	30 Lib	30 Sco	29 Sag	28 Cap
		30 Cap		30 Ari		30 Can	31 Vir				31 Aqu
BORN IN THE YEAR 1998											
2 Pis	2 Tau	2 Tau	2 Can	2 Leo	3 Lib	3 Sco	2 Sag	3 Aqu	2 Pis	1 Ari	2 Gem
4 Ari	4 Gem	4 Gem	4 Leo	4 Vir	5 Sco	5 Sag	4 Cap	5 Pis	4 Ari	3 Tau	4 Can
6 Tau	7 Can	6 Can	7 Vir	7 Lib	8 Sag	8 Cap	6 Aqu	7 Ari	6 Tau	5 Gem	6 Leo
8 Gem	9 Leo	8 Leo	9 Lib	9 Sco	10 Cap	10 Aqu	8 Pis	9 Tau	8 Gem	7 Can	9 Vir
10 Can	11 Vir	11 Vir	12 Sco	12 Sag	13 Aqu	12 Pis	11 Ari	11 Gem	10 Can	9 Leo	11 Lib
13 Leo	14 Lib	13 Lib	14 Sag	14 Cap	15 Pis	14 Ari	13 Tau	13 Can	13 Leo	11 Vir	14 Sco
15 Vir	16 Sco	16 Sco	17 Cap	16 Aqu	17 Ari	16 Tau	15 Gem	15 Leo	15 Vir	14 Lib	16 Sag
18 Lib	19 Sag	18 Sag	19 Aqu	19 Pis	19 Tau	18 Gem	17 Can	18 Vir	17 Lib	16 Sco	19 Cap
20 Sco	21 Cap	21 Cap	21 Pis	21 Ari	21 Gem	21 Can	19 Leo	20 Lib	20 Sco	19 Sag	21 Aqu
23 Sag	23 Aqu	23 Aqu	23 Ari	23 Tau	23 Can	23 Leo	21 Vir	23 Sco	23 Sag	21 Cap	23 Pis
25 Cap	25 Pis	25 Pis	25 Tau	25 Gem	25 Leo	25 Vir	24 Lib	25 Sag	25 Cap	24 Aqu	25 Ari
27 Aqu	27 Ari	27 Ari	27 Gem	27 Can	28 Vir	28 Lib	26 Sco	28 Cap	27 Aqu	26 Pis	28 Tau
29 Pis		29 Tau	29 Leo	30 Lib	30 Sco	30 Sag	29 Sag	30 Aqu	30 Pis	28 Ari	30 Gem
31 Ari		31 Gem		31 Vir			31 Cap			30 Tau	

	JAN	FEB	MAR	APR	MAY	JUN	JUL	AUG	SEP	OCT	NOV	DEC
BORN IN THE YEAR 1999											
	1 Can	1 Vir	1 Vir	2 Sco	2 Sag	3 Aqu	2 Pis	1 Ari	2 Gem	1 Can	1 Vir	1 Lib
	3 Leo	4 Lib	3 Lib	4 Sag	4 Cap	5 Pis	5 Ari	3 Tau	4 Can	3 Leo	4 Lib	3 Sco
	5 Vir	6 Sco	6 Sco	7 Cap	7 Aqu	8 Ari	7 Tau	5 Gem	6 Leo	6 Sco	6 Sag
	7 Lib	9 Sag	8 Sag	9 Aqu	9 Pis	10 Tau	9 Gem	7 Can	8 Vir	8 Lib	9 Sag	8 Cap
	10 Sco	11 Cap	11 Cap	12 Pis	11 Ari	12 Gem	11 Can	9 Leo	10 Lib	10 Sco	11 Cap	11 Aqu
	12 Sag	14 Aqu	13 Aqu	14 Ari	13 Tau	14 Can	13 Leo	12 Vir	13 Sco	12 Sag	14 Aqu	13 Pis
	15 Cap	16 Pis	15 Pis	16 Tau	15 Gem	16 Leo	15 Vir	14 Lib	15 Sag	15 Cap	16 Pis	16 Ari
	17 Aqu	18 Ari	17 Ari	18 Gem	17 Can	18 Vir	17 Lib	16 Sco	18 Cap	17 Aqu	18 Ari	18 Tau
	19 Pis	20 Tau	19 Tau	20 Can	19 Leo	20 Lib	20 Sco	19 Sag	20 Aqu	20 Pis	21 Tau	20 Gem
	22 Ari	22 Gem	21 Gem	22 Leo	21 Vir	23 Sco	22 Sag	21 Cap	22 Pis	22 Ari	23 Gem	22 Can
	24 Tau	24 Can	23 Can	24 Vir	24 Lib	25 Sag	25 Cap	24 Aqu	25 Ari	24 Tau	25 Can	24 Leo
	26 Gem	26 Leo	26 Leo	27 Lib	26 Sco	28 Cap	27 Aqu	26 Pis	27 Tau	26 Gem	27 Leo	26 Vir
	28 Can		28 Vir	29 Sco	29 Sag	30 Aqu	30 Pis	28 Ari	29 Gem	28 Can	29 Vir	28 Lib
	30 Leo		30 Lib		31 Cap			30 Tau				31 Sco
BORN IN THE YEAR 2000											
	3 Sag	1 Cap	2 Aqu	1 Pis	3 Tau	1 Gem	2 Leo	1 Vir	2 Sco	1 Sag	3 Aqu	2 Pis
	5 Cap	4 Aqu	4 Pis	3 Ari	5 Gem	3 Can	4 Vir	3 Lib	4 Sag	4 Cap	5 Pis	5 Ari
	7 Aqu	6 Pis	7 Ari	5 Tau	7 Can	5 Leo	7 Lib	5 Sco	6 Cap	6 Aqu	8 Ari	7 Tau
	10 Pis	8 Ari	9 Tau	7 Gem	9 Leo	7 Vir	9 Sco	8 Sag	9 Aqu	9 Pis	10 Tau	9 Gem
	12 Ari	11 Tau	11 Gem	9 Can	11 Vir	9 Lib	11 Sag	10 Cap	11 Pis	11 Ari	12 Gem	11 Can
	14 Tau	13 Gem	13 Can	11 Leo	13 Lib	12 Sco	14 Cap	13 Aqu	14 Ari	13 Tau	14 Can	13 Leo
	16 Gem	15 Can	15 Leo	14 Vir	15 Sco	14 Sag	16 Aqu	15 Pis	16 Tau	16 Gem	16 Leo	15 Vir
	18 Can	17 Leo	17 Vir	16 Lib	18 Sag	17 Cap	19 Pis	18 Ari	18 Gem	18 Can	18 Vir	18 Lib
	20 Leo	19 Vir	20 Lib	18 Sco	20 Cap	19 Aqu	21 Ari	20 Tau	20 Can	20 Leo	20 Lib	20 Sco
	23 Vir	21 Lib	22 Sco	21 Sag	23 Aqu	22 Pis	24 Tau	22 Gem	23 Leo	22 Vir	23 Sco	22 Sag
	25 Lib	23 Sco	24 Sag	23 Cap	25 Pis	24 Ari	26 Gem	24 Can	25 Vir	24 Lib	25 Sag	25 Cap
	27 Sco	26 Sag	27 Cap	26 Aqu	28 Ari	26 Tau	28 Can	26 Leo	27 Lib	26 Sco	27 Cap	27 Aqu
	29 Sag	28 Cap	29 Aqu	28 Pis	30 Tau	28 Gem	30 Leo	28 Vir	29 Sco	29 Sag	30 Aqu	30 Pis
				30 Ari		30 Can		30 Lib		31 Cap		
BORN IN THE YEAR 2001											
	1 Ari	2 Gem	1 Gem	2 Leo	1 Vir	2 Sco	1 Sag	3 Agu	1 Pis	1 Ari	2 Gem	2 Can
	4 Tau	4 Can	4 Can	4 Vir	3 Lib	4 Sag	4 Cap	5 Pis	4 Ari	4 Tau	4 Can	4 Leo
	6 Gem	6 Leo	6 Leo	6 Lib	6 Sco	7 Cap	6 Aqu	8 Ari	6 Tau	6 Gem	7 Leo	6 Vir
	8 Can	8 Vir	8 Vir	8 Sco	8 Sag	9 Aqu	9 Pis	10 Tau	9 Gem	8 Can	9 Vir	8 Lib
	10 Leo	10 Lib	10 Lib	10 Sag	10 Cap	11 Pis	11 Ari	12 Gem	11 Can	10 Leo	11 Lib	10 Sco
	12 Vir	12 Sco	12 Sco	13 Cap	13 Aqu	14 Ari	14 Tau	15 Can	13 Leo	13 Vir	13 Sco	12 Sag
	14 Lib	15 Sag	14 Sag	15 Aqu	15 Pis	16 Tau	16 Gem	17 Leo	15 Vir	15 Lib	15 Sag	15 Cap
	16 Sco	17 Cap	16 Cap	18 Pis	18 Ari	19 Gem	18 Can	19 Vir	17 Lib	17 Sco	17 Cap	17 Aqu
	18 Sag	20 Aqu	19 Aqu	20 Ari	20 Tau	21 Can	20 Leo	21 Lib	19 Sco	19 Sag	20 Aqu	20 Pis
	21 Cap	22 Pis	22 Pis	23 Tau	22 Gem	23 Leo	22 Vir	23 Sco	21 Sag	21 Cap	22 Pis	22 Ari
	23 Aqu	25 Ari	24 Ari	25 Gem	24 Can	25 Vir	24 Lib	25 Sag	24 Cap	23 Aqu	25 Ari	25 Tau
	26 Pis	27 Tau	26 Tau	27 Can	27 Leo	27 Lib	26 Sco	27 Cap	26 Aqu	26 Pis	27 Tau	27 Gem
	28 Ari		29 Gem	29 Leo	29 Vir	29 Sag	30 Aqu	29 Pis	28 Ari	30 Gem	29 Can
	31 Tau		31 Can		31 Lib		31 Cap			31 Tau		31 Leo
BORN IN THE YEAR 2002											
	2 Vir	1 Lib	2 Sco	1 Sag	2 Aqu	1 Pis	1 Ari	2 Gem	1 Can	1 Leo	1 Lib	1 Sco
	4 Lib	3 Sco	4 Sag	3 Cap	5 Pis	4 Ari	4 Tau	5 Can	3 Leo	3 Vir	3 Sco	3 Sag
	6 Sco	5 Sag	6 Cap	5 Aqu	7 Ari	6 Tau	6 Gem	7 Leo	5 Vir	5 Lib	5 Sag	5 Cap
	9 Sag	7 Cap	9 Aqu	8 Pis	10 Tau	9 Gem	8 Can	9 Vir	7 Lib	7 Sco	7 Cap	7 Aqu
	11 Cap	10 Aqu	11 Pis	10 Ari	12 Gem	11 Can	11 Leo	11 Lib	9 Sco	9 Sag	10 Aqu	9 Pis
	13 Aqu	12 Pis	14 Ari	13 Tau	14 Can	13 Leo	13 Vir	13 Sco	12 Sag	11 Cap	12 Pis	12 Ari
	16 Pis	15 Ari	16 Tau	15 Gem	17 Leo	15 Vir	15 Lib	15 Sag	14 Cap	13 Aqu	15 Ari	14 Tau
	18 Ari	17 Tau	19 Gem	18 Can	19 Vir	18 Lib	17 Sco	18 Cap	16 Aqu	16 Pis	17 Tau	17 Gem
	21 Tau	20 Gem	21 Can	20 Leo	21 Lib	20 Sco	19 Sag	20 Aqu	18 Pis	18 Ari	20 Gem	19 Can
	23 Gem	22 Can	24 Leo	22 Vir	23 Sco	22 Sag	21 Cap	22 Pis	21 Ari	21 Tau	22 Can	22 Leo
	26 Can	24 Leo	26 Vir	24 Lib	25 Sag	24 Cap	24 Aqu	25 Ari	23 Tau	23 Gem	24 Leo	24 Vir
	28 Leo	26 Vir	28 Lib	26 Sco	28 Cap	26 Aqu	26 Pis	27 Tau	26 Gem	26 Can	27 Vir	26 Lib
	30 Vir	28 Lib	30 Sco	28 Sag	30 Aqu	29 Pis	28 Ari	30 Gem	29 Can	28 Leo	29 Lib	28 Sco
				30 Cap			31 Tau			30 Vir		30 Sag

JAN	FEB	MAR	APR	MAY	JUN	JUL	AUG	SEP	OCT	NOV	DEC
BORN IN THE YEAR 2003											
1 Cap	2 Pis	1 Pis	3 Tau	2 Gem	1 Can	1 Leo	2 Lib	2 Sag	1 Cap	2 Pis	2 Ari
3 Aqu	5 Ari	4 Ari	5 Gem	5 Can	4 Leo	3 Vir	4 Sco	4 Cap	4 Aqu	5 Ari	4 Tau
6 Pis	7 Tau	6 Tau	8 Can	7 Leo	6 Vir	5 Lib	6 Sag	6 Aqu	6 Pis	7 Tau	7 Gem
8 Ari	10 Gem	9 Gem	10 Leo	10 Vir	8 Lib	7 Sco	8 Cap	9 Pis	8 Ari	10 Gem	9 Can
11 Tau	12 Can	11 Can	12 Vir	12 Lib	10 Sco	10 Sag	10 Aqu	11 Ari	11 Tau	12 Can	12 Leo
13 Gem	14 Leo	14 Leo	14 Lib	14 Sco	12 Sag	12 Cap	12 Pis	13 Tau	13 Gem	15 Leo	14 Vir
16 Can	16 Vir	16 Vir	16 Sco	16 Sag	14 Cap	14 Aqu	15 Ari	16 Gem	16 Can	17 Vir	16 Lib
18 Leo	18 Lib	18 Lib	18 Sag	18 Cap	16 Aqu	16 Pis	17 Tau	18 Leo	18 Leo	19 Lib	19 Sco
20 Vir	21 Sco	20 Sco	20 Cap	20 Aqu	19 Pis	18 Ari	20 Gem	21 Leo	21 Vir	21 Sco	21 Sag
22 Lib	23 Sag	22 Sag	23 Aqu	22 Pis	21 Ari	21 Tau	22 Can	23 Vir	23 Lib	23 Sag	23 Cap
24 Sco	25 Cap	24 Cap	25 Pis	25 Ari	23 Tau	23 Gem	24 Leo	25 Lib	25 Sco	25 Cap	25 Aqu
26 Sag	27 Aqu	26 Aqu	27 Ari	27 Tau	26 Gem	26 Can	27 Vir	27 Sco	27 Sag	27 Aqu	27 Pis
29 Cap		29 Pis	30 Tau	30 Gem	28 Can	28 Leo	29 Lib	29 Cap	29 Cap	29 Pis	29 Ari
31 Aqu		31 Ari				30 Vir	31 Sco		31 Aqu		
BORN IN THE YEAR 2004											
1 Tau	2 Can	3 Leo	1 Vir	1 Lib	2 Sag	1 Cap	1 Pis	2 Tau	2 Gem	1 Can	1 Leo
3 Gem	4 Leo	5 Vir	4 Lib	3 Sco	4 Cap	3 Aqu	4 Ari	5 Gem	5 Can	3 Leo	3 Vir
6 Can	7 Vir	7 Lib	6 Sco	5 Sag	6 Aqu	5 Pis	6 Tau	7 Can	7 Leo	6 Vir	6 Lib
8 Leo	9 Lib	9 Sco	9 Sag	7 Cap	8 Pis	7 Ari	8 Gem	10 Leo	10 Vir	8 Lib	8 Sco
10 Vir	11 Sco	12 Sag	11 Cap	9 Aqu	10 Ari	10 Tau	11 Can	12 Vir	12 Lib	10 Sco	10 Sag
13 Lib	13 Sag	14 Cap	13 Aqu	11 Pis	12 Tau	12 Gem	13 Leo	14 Lib	14 Sco	13 Sag	12 Cap
15 Sco	15 Cap	16 Aqu	14 Pis	14 Ari	15 Gem	15 Can	16 Vir	17 Sco	16 Sag	15 Cap	14 Aqu
17 Sag	17 Aqu	18 Pis	16 Ari	16 Tau	17 Can	17 Leo	18 Lib	19 Sag	18 Cap	17 Aqu	16 Pis
19 Cap	20 Pis	20 Ari	19 Tau	19 Gem	20 Leo	20 Vir	20 Sco	21 Cap	20 Aqu	19 Pis	18 Ari
21 Aqu	22 Ari	23 Tau	21 Gem	21 Can	22 Vir	22 Lib	23 Sag	23 Aqu	23 Pis	21 Ari	21 Tau
23 Pis	24 Tau	25 Gem	24 Can	24 Leo	25 Lib	24 Sco	25 Cap	25 Pis	25 Ari	23 Tau	23 Gem
25 Ari	27 Gem	28 Can	26 Leo	26 Vir	27 Sco	27 Sag	27 Aqu	27 Ari	27 Tau	26 Gem	25 Can
28 Tau	29 Can	30 Leo	29 Vir	28 Lib	29 Sag	29 Cap	29 Pis	29 Tau	29 Gem	28 Can	28 Leo
30 Gem				31 Sco			31 Ari				31 Vir
BORN IN THE YEAR 2005											
2 Lib	1 Sco	2 Sag	3 Aqu	2 Pis	3 Tau	2 Gem	1 Can	2 Vir	2 Lib	1 Sco	2 Cap
4 Sco	3 Sag	4 Cap	5 Pis	4 Ari	5 Gem	5 Can	3 Leo	5 Lib	4 Sco	3 Sag	4 Aqu
6 Sag	5 Cap	6 Aqu	7 Ari	6 Tau	7 Can	7 Leo	6 Vir	7 Sco	7 Sag	5 Cap	7 Pis
8 Cap	7 Aqu	8 Pis	9 Tau	9 Gem	10 Leo	10 Vir	8 Lib	9 Sag	9 Cap	7 Aqu	9 Ari
10 Aqu	9 Pis	10 Ari	11 Gem	11 Can	12 Vir	12 Lib	11 Sco	12 Cap	11 Aqu	9 Pis	11 Tau
12 Pis	11 Ari	13 Tau	14 Can	14 Leo	15 Lib	15 Sco	13 Sag	14 Aqu	13 Pis	11 Ari	13 Gem
15 Ari	13 Tau	15 Gem	16 Leo	16 Vir	17 Sco	17 Sag	15 Cap	16 Pis	15 Ari	14 Tau	15 Can
17 Tau	16 Gem	17 Can	19 Vir	18 Lib	19 Sag	19 Cap	17 Aqu	18 Ari	17 Tau	16 Gem	18 Leo
19 Gem	18 Can	20 Leo	21 Lib	21 Sco	21 Cap	21 Aqu	19 Pis	20 Tau	19 Gem	18 Can	20 Vir
22 Can	21 Leo	22 Vir	23 Sco	23 Sag	23 Aqu	23 Pis	21 Ari	22 Gem	22 Can	21 Leo	23 Lib
24 Leo	23 Vir	25 Lib	26 Sag	25 Cap	25 Pis	25 Ari	23 Tau	24 Can	24 Leo	23 Vir	25 Sco
27 Vir	25 Lib	27 Sco	28 Cap	27 Aqu	28 Ari	27 Tau	26 Gem	27 Leo	27 Vir	26 Lib	28 Sag
29 Lib	28 Sco	29 Sag	30 Aqu	29 Pis	30 Tau	29 Gem	28 Can	29 Vir	29 Lib	28 Sco	30 Cap
		31 Cap		31 Ari			31 Leo			30 Sag	
BORN IN THE YEAR 2006											
1 Aqu	1 Ari	1 Ari	1 Gem	1 Can	2 Vir	2 Lib	1 Sco	2 Cap	1 Aqu	2 Ari	1 Tau
3 Pis	3 Tau	3 Tau	4 Can	3 Leo	5 Lib	5 Sco	3 Sag	4 Aqu	4 Pis	4 Tau	3 Gem
5 Ari	6 Gem	5 Gem	6 Leo	6 Vir	7 Sco	7 Sag	6 Cap	6 Pis	6 Ari	6 Gem	6 Can
7 Tau	8 Can	7 Can	9 Vir	8 Lib	10 Sag	9 Cap	8 Aqu	8 Ari	8 Tau	8 Can	8 Leo
9 Gem	10 Leo	10 Leo	11 Lib	11 Sco	12 Cap	11 Aqu	10 Pis	10 Tau	10 Gem	10 Leo	10 Vir
12 Can	13 Vir	12 Vir	14 Sco	13 Sag	14 Aqu	13 Pis	12 Ari	12 Gem	12 Can	13 Vir	13 Lib
14 Leo	16 Lib	15 Lib	16 Sag	15 Cap	16 Pis	15 Ari	14 Tau	14 Can	14 Leo	15 Lib	15 Sco
17 Vir	18 Sco	17 Sco	18 Cap	18 Aqu	18 Ari	17 Tau	16 Gem	17 Leo	17 Vir	18 Sco	18 Sag
19 Lib	20 Sag	20 Sag	20 Aqu	20 Pis	20 Tau	20 Gem	18 Can	19 Vir	19 Lib	20 Sag	20 Cap
22 Sco	23 Cap	22 Cap	22 Pis	22 Ari	22 Gem	22 Can	21 Leo	22 Lib	22 Sco	23 Cap	22 Aqu
24 Sag	25 Aqu	24 Aqu	25 Ari	24 Tau	25 Can	24 Leo	23 Vir	24 Sco	24 Sag	25 Aqu	24 Pis
26 Cap	27 Pis	26 Pis	27 Tau	26 Gem	27 Leo	27 Vir	26 Lib	27 Sag	26 Cap	27 Pis	27 Ari
28 Aqu		28 Ari	29 Gem	28 Can	29 Vir	29 Lib	28 Sco	29 Cap	29 Aqu	29 Ari	29 Tau
30 Pis		30 Tau		31 Leo		31 Sag	31 Sag		31 Pis		31 Gem

WHAT YOUR MOON SIGN SAYS ABOUT YOU

Now that you know your Moon sign, read on to learn more about your emotional nature and your basic inner needs.

MOON IN ARIES

You have an emotional need to be first. And you want to be first *now* – there's no time to waste. Brimming with enthusiasm and energy, you love to keep busy and find waiting difficult. Remember to open up and talk to those closest to you about your feelings – they can help you to slow down and deal with any difficult emotions as they arise.

MOON IN TAURUS

You love to be surrounded by beautiful possessions and enjoy food and clothes that make you feel good – you have a need for comfort. Familiarity and routine are important to you, and you don't deal well with sudden change. That stubborn streak means you're able to stand up for yourself and protect your own interests, just remember to relax once in a while and try new things.

MOON IN GEMINI

Self-expression is one of your driving forces with this mix. Talking, drawing, writing – you simply have to communicate your feelings. And you love to listen to other peoples' ideas, too. To feed your curious intellect, you've probably got a tower of books and magazines at your bedside. Just don't forget to exercise your body as well as your mind.

MOON IN CANCER

You were born to nurture others – whether that's through baking them a cake or being at the end of the phone when they need your reassuring words. Family is hugely important to you, and you want to feel loved and secure. Being honest about this and accepting your wonderfully sensitive and emotional nature will help you find inner peace.

MOON IN LEO

You have an emotional need to be admired – all you really want is for everyone to love you. Your kind heart and generosity towards your friends and family means you are usually surrounded by others, and the attention you crave is easily won. When things don't go your way, you have a tendency to be dramatic – don't let your pride stop you from asking for help when you need it.

MOON IN VIRGO

You are a gentle soul and appreciate the simple things in life. Helping others in small ways makes you feel needed, secure and purposeful. A clean and tidy environment is a must, and everything has to be in its proper place. Learning not to fuss when something isn't perfect is a challenge – look for useful ways to keep your practical nature busy and happiness will follow.

MOON IN LIBRA

Close bonds are everything to you – you find strength and stability in your relationships with others. Your need for balance and harmony means you are an excellent peacemaker, skilled at helping people to see and understand another's perspective. Remember to feed your love of beauty with regular trips to art galleries and picturesque places.

MOON IN SCORPIO

Deep and emotionally intense, you need to trust those close to you with your innermost thoughts and desires. All or nothing, you have incredible intuition and can see right to the heart of people. Finding one or two close friends who you can really open up to and be honest with about your feelings is important for your happiness. When this happens, your inner strength is unmatched.

MOON IN SAGITTARIUS

Your need for freedom and space is overwhelming, but when you achieve it, you are bright, breezy and filled with a zest for life. Always on the lookout for new things to try and people to meet, your energy and enthusiasm lifts the spirits of those around you. Planning is not your strong suit; you prefer to go with the flow and see where it takes you – preferably somewhere fun and interesting!

MOON IN CAPRICORN

Ambitious and practical, you want to work hard and achieve results. You are conscientious and naturally organized, with a clear picture of what you want and how you intend to get there. Remember to take time to kick back and relax – the strong front you present to those around you can hide your more sensitive side. Letting go occasionally isn't a sign of weakness.

MOON IN AQUARIUS

Your desire to be unique and unusual is powerful, and you need the space and freedom to be yourself. Emotionally detached, you are happily independent and have an ability to see the bigger picture. Try not to lose touch with those closest to you – life is full of ups and downs, and friends and family can offer valuable support through tougher times.

MOON IN PISCES

Dreamy and intuitive, your sensitive nature is highly attuned to the feelings of others. Be careful to steer clear of negative people – you're likely to absorb their vibes, and they will bring you down. It's important you learn how to take care of yourself when you feel overwhelmed emotionally. Escaping into a good book or listening to your favourite music can be a great way to re-set.

YOUR ELEMENTAL TYPE

Fire, Earth, Air, Water – in ancient times these were thought to contain everything that existed on Earth. Today that's no longer the case, but there's no denying their powerful effect on people's lives. Think of the heat from the Sun, the way earth is used to grow food, the water you consume, the air that you breathe. And like so much in astrology, each element has two sides. You drink water and rain helps plants to grow, but the force of a tsunami can wreak havoc and destruction. You have all four elements within you, but one or more of them will stand out. You could be a single type, or a mix of two or three. Your elemental type says a lot about you and those you interact with. When you meet someone you feel naturally comfortable with, it's often because you are elementally compatible.

IN YOUR ELEMENT

Capricorn is the most go-getting of the Earth signs, especially when it comes to practical matters. You know what you want, and you're prepared to put in the work to get there. You want to be the boss, and have the drive and ambition to make this happen. At your best, you are a force to be reckoned with, hugely proactive and able to plan years in advance; at your worst, you are so caught up in those plans you forget to stop and enjoy life along the way.

 ## EARTH WITH FIRE

Not ideally compatible, as Earth extinguishes Fire, while 'scorched Earth' is sterile and unproductive. Still, Fire can get you going, energizing you with its passion and intensity, while you can slow Fire down, acting as a grounding force.

 ## EARTH WITH EARTH

Stable and peaceful, you are very compatible, bolstering each other's strengths. Watch out you don't get stuck in the same routine, or focus so much on the practical side of things you forget to let loose and have some fun.

 ## EARTH WITH AIR

Not an ideal mix. Air wants excitement rather than stability, and Earth can feel irritated by Air's flightiness. You do challenge each other to think differently and see things from a new perspective, but ultimately Earth can find Air exhausting.

 ## EARTH WITH WATER

Comfortable and secure, you work wonderfully together, each helping the other to reach their potential. You are Water's rock, grounding them emotionally and helping them to get things done, while Water refreshes and enlivens you.

THE MISSING PIECE

How dominant Earth is within you depends on the influence of the other elements in your chart – ideally all four would be represented. Sometimes a lack of a particular element can cause an imbalance, making you feel rundown or stressed. The best way to counteract this is to tune in to the missing element and reharmonize yourself. Try the simple exercise below to get back in touch with any elements you're missing.

1. First, take a look at the Zodiac signs and their elements.

Fire: Aries, Leo, Sagittarius

Earth: Taurus, Virgo, Capricorn

Air: Gemini, Libra, Aquarius

Water: Cancer, Scorpio, Pisces

2. Now circle Earth, as this is the element that represents your Sun sign. You're certain to have some of this element. Then do the same for your Moon sign and your Ascendant, circling the element associated with each.

3. Looking at the list, there should be one or more elements you haven't circled.

Fire – not enough Fire can leave you lacking in energy and motivation. You want to be more assertive and prepared to take the lead.

Air – Air will help you to communicate better, feel more sociable and lift your spirits. Use it to boost your curiosity and sharpen your wits.

Water – with Water missing you may struggle to get in touch with your emotions or worry you're being insensitive. You're looking to express yourself, to feel more creative and inspired.

4. Choose the element you would like to tune in to, whichever one you feel might benefit you. Then pick one of the ideas from the lists below. If Fire is missing, you could turn your face to the sun and soak up its warmth. If it's Water, you could try a soak in the tub. You can use this exercise whenever you feel out of balance.

FIRE

Sunbathe
Toast marshmallows
Watch fireworks
Host a barbecue
Meditate on a candle flame
Catch the sunrise
Go stargazing

AIR

Fly a kite
Watch clouds go by
Blow bubbles
Feel the breeze
Breathe deep
Play with a balloon
Chase butterflies

WATER

Spend a day at the beach
Splash in a puddle
Sit by a fountain
Walk in the rain
Catch a wave
Snorkel

We are
FAMILY

WE'RE ALL IN THIS TOGETHER

When so much in your life is changing, your relationships with your parents can become even more important. If you're lucky, you get on well with yours, but even the most harmonious relationships can come under strain during the teenage years. How can astrology help? It can remind you that parents are people, too. They might not get everything right, but hopefully you believe that they have your best interests at heart. Learning more about who they are, why they do things and how you relate to them can make it easier for all of you to move forwards together.

MOTHER MOON

The Moon sign you are born with can tell you a lot about how you see and treat your mother. This is because your Moon sign represents your emotional needs – what you need to feel safe and secure – and these are most often fulfilled by your mother. How you react to her can make a big difference to the way she behaves around you. If you are visibly upset by certain things she does, she is likely to change her behaviour the next time around. If you react with happiness and delight, she is more likely to repeat them.

Here's how you see your mother according to your Moon sign . . .

ARIES

You view your mother as strong, honest and forthright. Sometimes, especially when she doesn't agree with your plans, this can make you feel as though she's taking over. Try not to push back too strongly, and remember she has your interests at heart.

TAURUS

You like to feel your mother is looking after all of your everyday needs and is dependable and reliable. Don't judge her too harshly if she doesn't always live up to your expectations – providing for others is often a careful balancing act, and she is likely doing her best.

GEMINI

Flighty and impulsive, you need your mother to give you the freedom to be yourself and make your own mistakes. Space and independence often have to be earned, though – what could you do to show her you're capable and trustworthy?

CANCER

Your longing for your mother's emotional attention can give you a wonderful bond and connection. However, the slightest hint of rejection from her can wound you deeply. Try not to take her reactions personally – it's okay for her to make choices and have goals that differ from yours.

LEO

You want to enjoy an open, honest relationship with your mother, where both of you say what you mean. Underlying this candour is a need for assurance and acceptance – when you feel vulnerable, be brave and explain to her how you feel.

VIRGO

You are aware of who gives what in your emotional relationship with your mother, and occasionally this can make you feel that she isn't there for you. Viewing her actions as 'different' rather than 'wrong' will help you to trust she is doing what she thinks is right.

LIBRA

You need your mother to recognize your emotional needs as valid and important. Try not to spend too much time putting others first – your relationship will flourish when you both accept the roles you play.

SCORPIO

You want your mother to respect your emotional boundaries and allow you alone-time when you need it. The trust between you can be intense and unconditional, so much so you may have to remind her to step back occasionally.

SAGITTARIUS

Upbeat and curious, your relationship works best when your mother is inspiring and encouraging, giving you the emotional freedom you need to expand your horizons. It's fine to chase independence, as long as you respect your mother's desire to give you roots.

CAPRICORN

You empathize strongly with your mother's feelings, so when she's struggling, this can make you feel it's your fault. Learn to let go of this guilt – it's unintentional and unhelpful. Instead, recognize how much you need each other's emotional support and encouragement.

AQUARIUS

You're not sure your mother's attempts to guide you are always necessary, and you don't like to burden her with your problems. Asking for help and talking things through might be more useful than you imagine and can bring you closer together at the same time.

PISCES

Your mother's high expectations have made you stronger emotionally, even though there are times when you just want to feel like a child and let her take care of everything. Taking responsibility can be tough; don't be afraid to speak up when you need support.

HOW YOU SEE YOUR FATHER

Just as your Moon sign gives you an indication of how you see your mother, or whoever plays that nurturing role in your life, your Sun sign can reveal the way you view your father, or the caregiver who is most involved with discipline. Your relationship with this person is built over time. For girls, it can have a strong bearing on how you view any future romantic relationships, whereas boys will either rebel or identify with these traits.

With the Sun in Capricorn, you see your father as strong and self-disciplined. Naturally, he's keen to pass on these traits to you, too. He also teaches you the importance of respect. Although he's not the type of father to take you white-water rafting, he happily plans outings with an educational twist, making sure you both have fun along the way.

Now read on to find out how your father's Sun sign affects your relationship . . .

Your father's Sun sign will play a significant part in how you relate to him, and it can help you to understand why he acts the way he does – however infuriating it may sometimes seem!

ARIES

While an Aries parent might seem a little hands-off in their approach, it's probably because they have a firm belief you're going to go places in life. If, however, you need a little reassurance sometimes, don't be afraid to ask for it.

TAURUS

The pair of you are incredibly single-minded, strictly focusing on one thing at a time. You might not always be on the same wavelength when it comes to physical affection – don't be embarrassed to ask your dad for a hug occasionally.

GEMINI

A mix of these two can bring tension because Earth and Air signs often find it hard to achieve a balance. Capricorn wants stability, while Gemini thrives on the unknown. It might help to try stepping into each other's shoes occasionally.

CANCER

As opposite signs of the Zodiac, your practical nature can sometimes seem at odds with your dad's feelings-led approach. If your dad can focus on home life and leave you to deal with your own finances, harmony reigns.

LEO

Your sometimes serious nature is softened by Leo's bubbly attitude. It's likely that you'll work with this energy throughout your life, especially when you hit bumpy patches. Humour is the secret to your lasting success.

VIRGO

Although you are both Earth signs, often known for their honesty, you can find it difficult to express your feelings to each other. Exploring the more practical things you have in common – work interests, for example – can help to guide you both.

LIBRA

Capricorn often believes hard work is the secret to life, while Libra has a more laid-back view. Your relationship can hit speed bumps because of this difference, but if you agree you're headed in the same direction, you'll be able to keep going.

SCORPIO

There's a basis for true understanding between you and your dad. While you might put on a different face to the outside world, when you are alone, it can seem easy. You could even end up going into business together.

SAGITTARIUS

You can sometimes find it hard to connect with each other. Capricorn has a wise, old-soul quality that a firecracker Sagittarius doesn't immediately understand. But don't worry, the relationship is likely to flourish as you get older.

CAPRICORN

Your father might have struggled with shyness as a child, but this is likely to make him your biggest cheerleader when you're making new friends. He does like things done 'my way or the highway', but you know how to charm him (mostly).

AQUARIUS

You could be the most organized parent/child combination in the Zodiac. At Christmas, you probably exchange planners for the coming year. Learning to be more spontaneous could take your relationship to the next level.

PISCES

Sometimes it might feel like you're the one setting the boundaries – your dad isn't even sure what they are! The good news is, you're more than capable and only too happy to step up when it's needed.

FRIENDS FOR LIFE

Friends play an essential role in your happiness. They can help you to move forwards when times are tough, see things from a new perspective and encourage you just to have fun. Every good friend you make has different qualities that will influence you and allow you to make more of your potential. A friend might show you it can be better to hold back when all you want to do is rush in, motivate you to stick with that project right to the end or inspire you to see an obstacle as a challenge. And astrology can be a great way to highlight those characteristics you're looking for in a friend. It can also tell you more about the type of friend you make for others.

WHAT KIND OF FRIEND ARE YOU?

Once you let your guard down, you're a warm, loving and faithful friend, but it can be a slow process. You mean the best, but you can sometimes be misjudged as aloof or unfriendly and, likewise, you aren't always a good judge of character. When you find the right match, however, you'll show total devotion, even in the bad times. You've got a sly sense of humour, too.

Strengths: *Responsible, supportive, faithful*
Weaknesses: *Condescending, standoffish, serious*
Friendship style: *Thoughtful, rational, work hard/play hard*

IF YOUR BEST FRIEND IS . . .

ARIES

Aries make friends easily. They're willing to help you achieve your goals, they see the best in you and they're happy to take risks for you, too. They love to be someone's best friend and can find it difficult to feel second to anyone else. They are always on the lookout for new, super-fun adventures and are happy to take you along for the ride. They have a knack for bringing people from all walks of life together.

Strengths: *Loyal, generous, fun-loving*
Weaknesses: *Insensitive, demanding, petulant*
Friendship style: *Busy, fun, warm*

TAURUS

Considerate and charming, Taurus friends often have a talent for giving good advice. They like to take their time and allow friendships to develop slowly, but once you become close they treat you as a member of their family. As an Earth sign, they are dependable and grounded, and they make wonderful lifelong friends. Bear in mind they can place too much importance on material possessions, even judging others based on their wealth.

Strengths: *Caring, faithful, trustworthy*
Weaknesses: *Judgmental, stubborn, materialistic*
Friendship style: *Helpful, sweet, self-assured*

GEMINI

You'll need lots of energy to keep up with a Gemini friend. They love to have fun, do crazy things and always have a story to tell. They'll make you laugh, but they can sometimes get a little carried away, perhaps exaggerating tales of their adventures in their effort to entertain you. They can be a bit gossipy, but they're not malicious. They're good listeners and will make you feel great, giving you lots of compliments – and always genuine ones, too.

Strengths: *Intelligent, energetic, fearless*
Weaknesses: *Impatient, easily bored, gossipy*
Friendship style: *Good listener, witty, spontaneous*

CANCER

Once you form a close connection with Cancer, you have a friend who has your back. They're considerate and like nothing better than to make you feel happy. Watch out though; they're deeply emotional, which means that if you fall out – even over something small – you'll have to work hard to patch things up again.

Strengths: *Loving, caring, intuitive*
Weaknesses: *Unforgiving, anxious, sensitive*
Friendship style: *Warm, affectionate, protective*

LEO

As long as you don't expect too much from a Leo friend, you're in for a treat. Outgoing, confident and full of energy, they thrive on social occasions and love to be the life and soul of a party, making people laugh and being admired. They're good at bringing people together and are in high demand, so you won't always have them to yourself, but if you can tie them down, you'll have some great quality one-on-one time.

Strengths: *Honest, brave, positive*
Weaknesses: *Arrogant, self-centred, proud*
Friendship style: *Supportive, cheerful, humorous*

VIRGO

With a Virgo by your side you'll always have somewhere to go when times are tough. They'll be there for you, giving you well-thought-out advice and a gentle sympathetic ear. Even when there's not a crisis, they're charming and kind. They like to be organized, so if they make plans, make sure you stick to them. They won't let you down, but they'll expect the same from you in return.

Strengths: *Warm, modest, smart*
Weaknesses: *Shy, serious, overly critical*
Friendship style: *Fixer, good communicator, reliable*

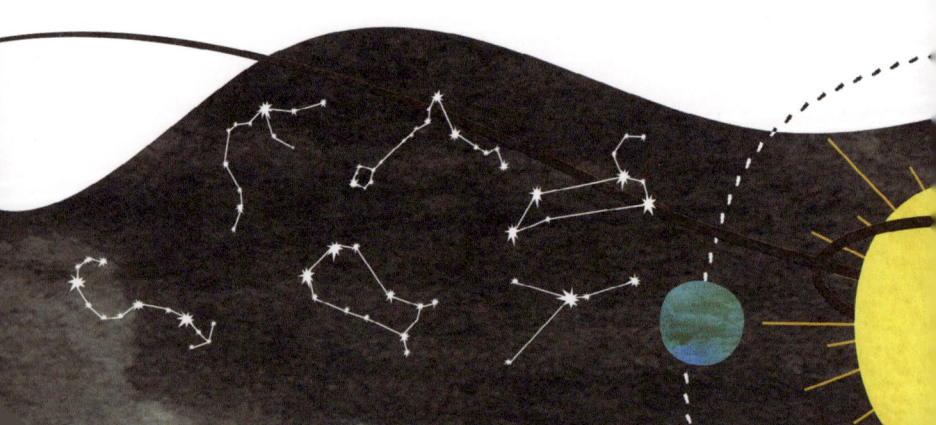

LIBRA

You can rely on your Libra friend to tell you how it is. They have a refreshing honesty, but they have a diplomatic way of sparing your feelings. They love spending time with you and like nothing better than a chat (especially if they're the one doing the talking!). They can always see both sides, so if there's a disagreement, it won't be for long.

Strengths: *Diplomatic, honest, sociable*
Weaknesses: *Indecisive, people pleaser, chatterbox*
Friendship style: *Laid-back, devoted, forgiving*

SCORPIO

It's an honour to be a Scorpio's best friend. They're selective, so they don't always have many, but the friendships they do make will be really special. Once you've cemented your friendship, they'll open their inner circle to you and will want to spend lots of time together. In return, they'll expect 100 per cent loyalty and might not take it well if you let them down, so tread carefully.

Strengths: *Passionate, hospitable, perceptive*
Weaknesses: *Guarded, jealous, suspicious*
Friendship style: *Intense, selective, highly loyal*

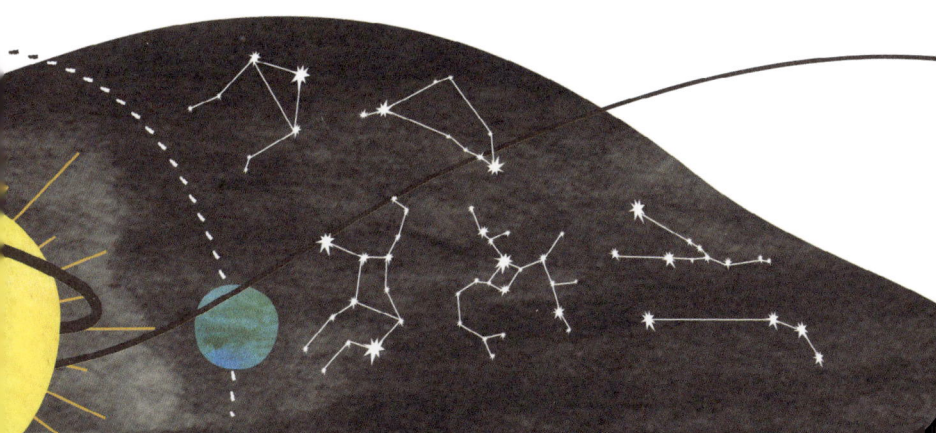

SAGITTARIUS

Sagittarius are low-maintenance friends. Easy-going, positive and happy-go-lucky, they're up for anything. If you fancy an adventure, give them a call, but don't expect too much of them emotions-wise. Their friendship circle is wide and diverse, so you'll get to meet lots of interesting people, but they are easily bored and can struggle with emotional closeness. On the plus side, they won't put too many demands on you, so give them some space and enjoy the ride.

Strengths: *Adventurous, positive, open-minded*
Weaknesses: *Impatient, insensitive, easily bored*
Friendship style: *Generous, undemanding, never dull*

AQUARIUS

You'll have to share your Aquarius best friend – they'll probably flit in and out of lots of other friendships, too – but rest assured they've got your back and will go to the ends of the earth for you. They'll bring plenty of excitement and fun into your world, but they also treasure their alone time, so don't put too many demands on them. They'll never pass judgment on you, no matter what you do.

Strengths: *Tolerant, independent, energetic*
Weaknesses: *Easily bored, rebellious, forgetful*
Friendship style: *Fun, exciting, unpredictable*

PISCES

A Pisces friend is a great listener who is sympathetic and caring and will always make time for you. They're the perfect friend if you need a shoulder to cry on, but they can sometimes get too emotionally involved. If there is any discord in your friendship, they are quick to blame themselves. Reassure them and let them know it's not their fault and you'll soon win back their love and support.

Strengths: *Loving, caring, good listener*
Weaknesses: *Sensitive, self-pitying, insecure*
Friendship style: *Supportive, sympathetic, selfless*

Your BIRTHDAY log

List the birthdays of your family and friends and discover their Sun signs

ARIES

March 21–April 20

Passionate, energetic, impulsive

TAURUS

April 21–May 21

Steady, tenacious, trustworthy

GEMINI
May 22–June 21

Intelligent, outgoing, witty

CANCER

June 22–July 22

Caring, home-loving, affectionate

LEO

July 23–August 23

Loud, big-hearted, fun

VIRGO

August 24–September 22

Organized, modest, responsible

LIBRA

September 23–October 22

Charming, creative, graceful

SCORPIO

October 23–November 21

Powerful, mysterious, magnetic

SAGITTARIUS

November 22–December 21

Adventurous, optimistic, lucky

CAPRICORN

December 22–January 20

Ambitious, dedicated, serious

AQUARIUS

January 21–February 19

Eccentric, independent, imaginative

PISCES

February 20–March 20

Dreamy, sensitive, compassionate

Lucky in
LOVE

WHY OPPOSITES REALLY DO ATTRACT

The sign opposite your Ascendant (your Rising sign) on your birth chart reveals who you will attract, and who will attract you. Known as your Descendant, it's the constellation that was setting on the Western horizon at the moment and place you were born.

This sign is everything you are not – a kind of mirror image, or two sides of the same coin.

Yet, strangely, you are often drawn to the qualities of this sign over and over again in the people you meet. It's possible that these characteristics are ones you feel you lack yourself, and you sense that the other person can fill in what's missing. Sometimes it really is true that opposites attract!

Ascendant	Descendant
Aries	Libra
Taurus	Scorpio
Gemini	Sagittarius
Cancer	Capricorn
Leo	Aquarius
Virgo	Pisces
Libra	Aries
Scorpio	Taurus
Sagittarius	Gemini
Capricorn	Cancer
Aquarius	Leo
Pisces	Virgo

WHAT DO YOU LOOK FOR?

Once you've matched up your Ascendant with your Descendant from the list on the previous page, you can get to know the qualities that are most likely to attract you. You can use this information whether you're thinking about romance or friendship.

LIBRA DESCENDANT

You're looking for balance and harmony in your relationship, with someone who makes you feel interesting and important. You want to be listened to and value the ability to compromise. Gentleness and sensitivity are the qualities you're searching for.

SCORPIO DESCENDANT

You want an intense, passionate relationship with someone who will welcome you wholeheartedly into their world and want to spend lots of time with you. You are attracted to someone who will take control, but who will also look out for you and protect you.

SAGITTARIUS DESCENDANT

Adventure and fun are what you crave when it comes to love. You want someone open-minded who will accept you for who you are. You need to be given plenty of space to breathe and not be stifled by too many demands.

CAPRICORN DESCENDANT

You seek total dedication and devotion from those you love. You're happy to take your time and let a relationship develop naturally, and aren't put off by someone who appears cool or guarded. You like a cheeky sense of humour, too.

AQUARIUS DESCENDANT

You are attracted to someone who is independent and has a full life outside of your relationship, although you want to know that if push comes to shove, they will be right there for you. You like to be kept on your toes.

PISCES DESCENDANT

You're not afraid of a deep relationship with someone who wears their heart on their sleeve. You want to be cared for, emotionally supported and loved unconditionally. You want to be the centre of someone's world.

ARIES DESCENDANT

You like someone to spar with and who lets you have your own way, but is still strong enough to put their foot down when the gravity of the situation demands it. You will need to respect your partner's strength, bravery and integrity.

TAURUS DESCENDANT

Stability and reliability are high on your list of priorities when it comes to forming relationships. You dislike chaos and are drawn to people who you know won't surprise or disappoint you. Instead you want a partnership that's grounded and safe.

GEMINI DESCENDANT

You're attracted to someone who is spontaneous and fearless, and who can keep you entertained. You're likely to fall for someone who makes you feel super-special and is quick to recognize your achievements and boost your confidence.

CANCER DESCENDANT

You seek relationships where you're made to feel like one of the family, where your every need and demand is met, particularly emotionally. You want to feel warm and fuzzy and protected by those you love.

LEO DESCENDANT

You're drawn to someone who is strong, confident and outgoing with a busy social life but who can also give you warmth and passion when required. You're attracted to those who can make you laugh and sweep you off your feet.

VIRGO DESCENDANT

You long for kindness and tenderness in a partnership, along with reliability. You want someone who can bring order into your life and who will think things through in a methodical way. Nothing should be left to chance.

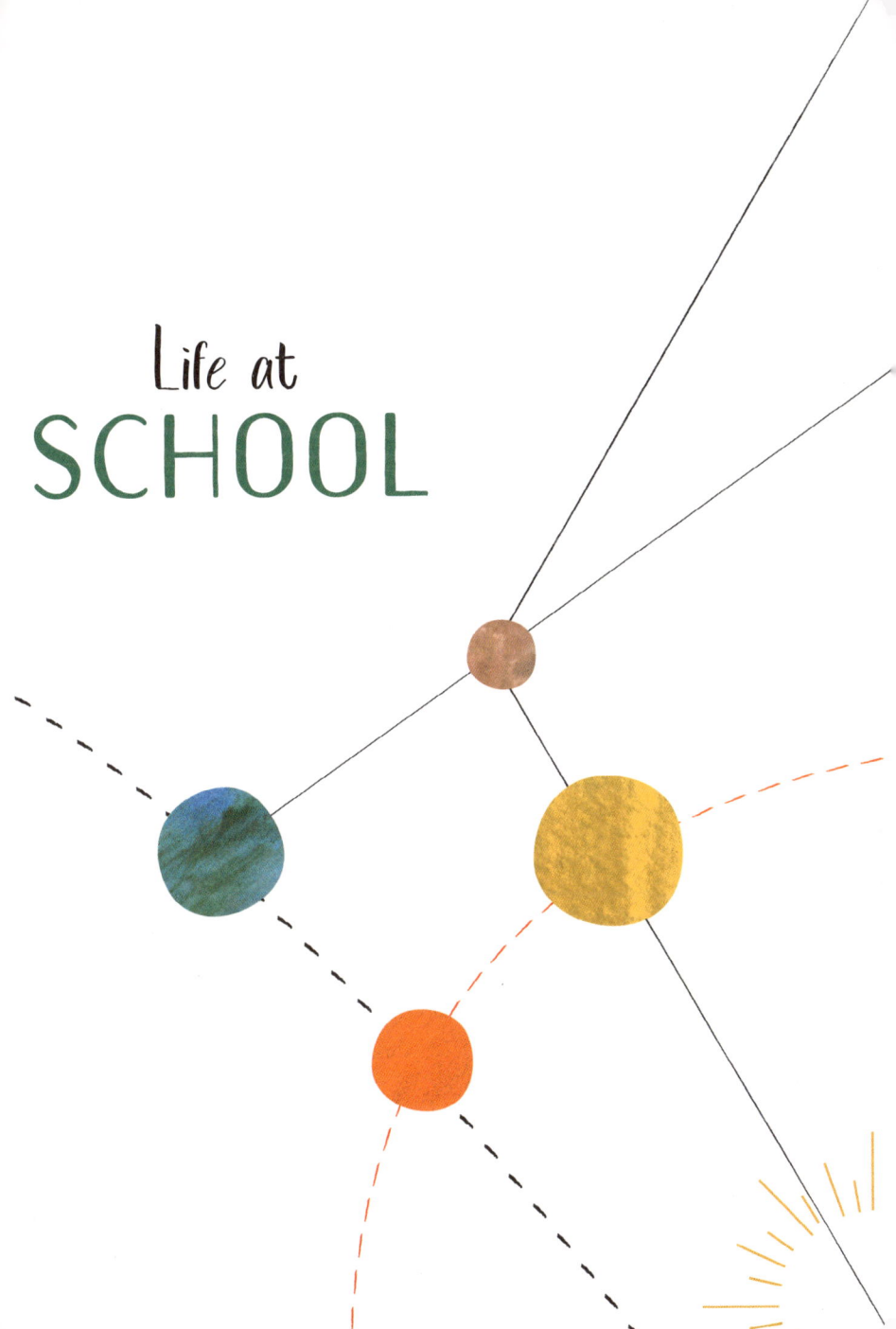

WORKING WONDERS

Have you ever been told that your years at school will be 'the best of your life'? Do you think they will be? Why? Many different things will determine how much you enjoy your school days. And there are sure to be ups and downs along the way. But there are a couple of important factors that astrology can help with. The first is determining your skills and strengths, and the second is learning to work well with others. Identifying your natural interests and abilities can help you to develop a sense of purpose, and it's this that is most likely to motivate you to work hard and actually have fun while you do it. To have a sense of purpose, you need to know yourself and what it is you want from your life. Not what others want for you, or what is expected of you, but what actually makes you come alive.

HIDDEN TALENTS

Not all of your attributes will be immediately obvious. Just because you're a Capricorn doesn't necessarily mean you always feel determined, for example. You can think about what a typical Capricorn might be good at, but you are unique, and the stars are only a guide. Think about your strengths – both emotional and physical. The examples on the right may strike a chord with you, or you might want to create your own list.

BECAUSE YOU'RE . . . CONSCIENTIOUS

You are responsible and hard-working, purposeful and determined. You tend to plan in advance and focus on finishing tasks that you've started. You feel bad when you don't manage to complete something.

Maybe you could be a . . .
lawyer, accountant, scientist

BECAUSE YOU'RE . . . ENERGETIC

You are a doer more than a thinker and take action to make things happen. Getting things done quickly and efficiently is important to you. You love to achieve things, have bundles of energy and work very hard.

Maybe you could be a . . .
estate agent, project manager, business developer

BECAUSE YOU'RE . . . ORGANIZED

You like to plan. You are well organized and good at sticking to deadlines, using targets and routines to get things done.

Maybe you could be a . . .
teacher, events manager, community organizer

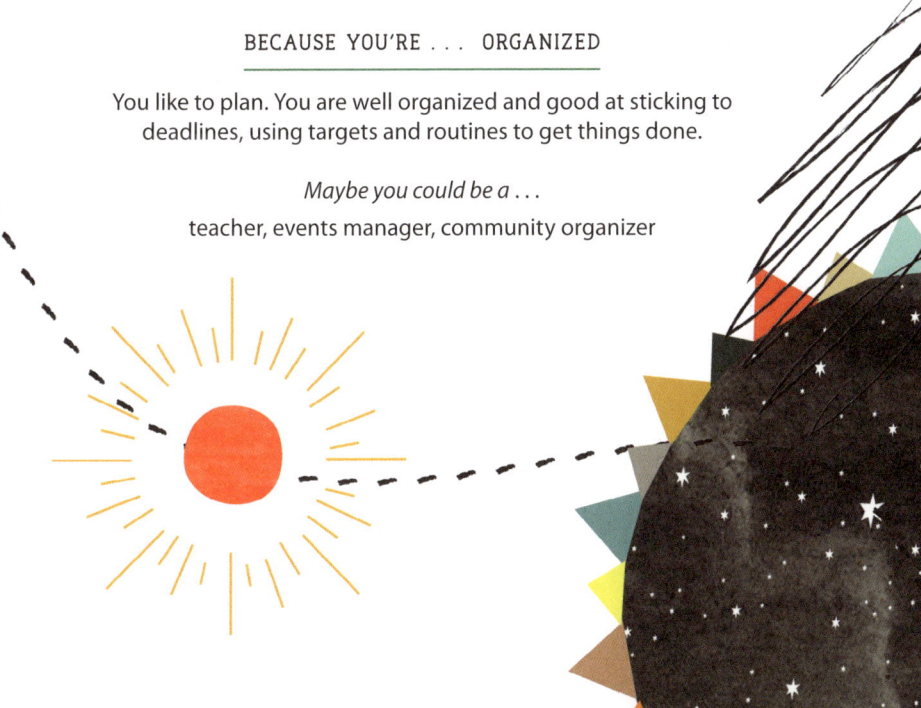

BECAUSE YOU'RE ... A LEADER

You love to persuade other people to do something, buy something or believe in your cause. You're great at influencing and motivating others.

Maybe you could be a ...
fundraiser, engineer, entrepreneur

BECAUSE YOU'RE ... DETERMINED

You enjoy completing tasks and persevere to finish what you started. You work hard to reach your goals and keep going even when things aren't working out.

Maybe you could be a ...
computer programmer, antiques dealer, headteacher

FAMOUS CAPRICORN PEOPLE

Henri Matisse – *Artist*
JRR Tolkien – *Author*
Joan of Arc – *Heroine and saint*
Stephen Hawking – *Theoretical physicist*
Elvis Presley – *Singer*
Kate Middleton – *Duchess of Cambridge*
Martin Luther King Jr – *Political figure and activist*
Michelle Obama – *Social activist and former First Lady*

TEAM WORK

Working together with others is essential for almost any career path you choose to follow in later life. School can be competitive, yet working in collaboration with your peers rather than against them builds skills that today's employers are looking for.

Here's how well you work together with . . .

ARIES

While you share an eagerness to succeed, you tend to take things slow and steady, so Aries' patience might be put to the test at times. However, you both love a challenge, especially in the workplace, and will put in 100 per cent effort all the way.

TAURUS

This hard-working team will get there eventually but in your own time. Together, you're unlikely to take risks but can be relied upon to meet the objective, give it your all and not complain. You're bound to become good friends, too.

GEMINI

As long as there's no rush to get things done and you respect each other's way of tackling things, you two should get along nicely. You both want to do a job well and feel a sense of achievement. You've got more in common than you think.

CANCER

While you will usually take the safer, steadier route and leave personal relationships aside, Cancer is very much ruled by emotions and treats the workplace like home. These two different perspectives can come together to give a wonderfully balanced view.

LEO

You two might never be the best of friends – you're just too different – but in the workplace you'll find a way of getting along. Let Leo do its lion thing – even if it might make you uncomfortable – and reassure Leo that boundaries don't necessarily mean cages.

VIRGO

You two are a great team. Neither of you are afraid of a bit of hard work and don't mind putting in some long hours, at the risk of being workaholics. You like to follow procedures and are disapproving of those who don't. Others might tell you to lighten up, but you're happy the way you are.

LIBRA

Libra will need to put in maximum effort to gain your respect, because you're a firm believer that only team players who work the hardest deserve to get ahead. In return, you will have to open your mind to their more relaxed approach. If this can be achieved, both sides will be much happier.

SCORPIO

Strong ambition on both sides will ensure this team will flourish. Your Scorpio colleague will come up with the strategic ideas, and you'll be there to give them structure. You would work well together on setting up a new venture and, in doing so, you'll likely end up lifelong friends.

SAGITTARIUS

You might struggle to see eye to eye when it comes to working practices. Your approaches are so dissimilar. Sagittarius will want to go out and explore an idea freely in the wider world, while you prefer to do it the 'proper' way, following the correct procedures. Hopefully you'll reach the same conclusion in the end.

CAPRICORN

This has the potential to be one of the most productive pairings provided you both agree on the end goal. Capricorn is one of the most ambitious signs in the Zodiac, so you're both prepared to put in the hours. You'll take your time, and you won't take too many risks, but you'll get excellent results.

AQUARIUS

You come at things from opposing angles – you're motivated by your own professional standing while Aquarius is motivated by the world at large. If you end up in a team together, you must make sure you have a clear objective. If not, you're going to find it hard to get off the starting block, let alone see the task through.

PISCES

Do you follow your head or your heart? That's the conundrum for you two. Find some middle ground, and you could make things happen. After all, you're both capable of seeing someone else's point of view. Go on, give it a try. If you don't, there'll be frustrations on both sides, and you might have to call it a day.

First published 2019
by Ammonite Press
an imprint of Guild of Master Craftsman Publications Ltd
Castle Place, 166 High Street, Lewes, East Sussex, BN7 1XU
United Kingdom

www.ammonitepress.com

Copyright in the Work © GMC Publications Ltd, 2019

Editorial: Susie Duff, Jane Roe, Rachel Roberts, Paul Wade
Designer: Jo Chapman
Illustrations: Sara Thielker
Cover illustration: Sara Thielker

ISBN 978-1-78145-403-9

All rights reserved

No part of this publication may be reproduced, stored in a retrieval system
or transmitted in any form or by any means (including electronic, mechanical, photocopying,
recording or otherwise) without prior written permission from the publisher

The publishers can accept no legal responsibility for any consequences arising from the
application of information, advice or instructions given in this publication

A catalogue record for this book is available from the British Library

Colour reproduction by GMC Reprographics
Printed and bound in China

AMMONITE
PRESS